SAY Insha Allah

Published by Ali Gator Productions.

First Published 2017

National Library of Australia Cataloguing-in-Publication (CIP) data:
Ahmad Zakky, Say Insha Allah
ISBN 978-1-921772-43-6
For primary school age, Juvenile fiction, Dewey Number: 823.92

T: +61 (3) 9386 2771 F: +61 (3) 9478 8854
P.O. Box 2536, Regent West, Melbourne Victoria, 3072 Australia
E: info@ali-gator.com W: www.ali-gator.com

Yasmeen and Abdul, with their two friends
Tasneem & Rafi had been playing
at the park all afternoon.

"It's getting late,
it's time to go home Abdul,"
said big sister Yasmeen.

"But it's still early, can't we play for longer?" asked Abdul.

"No, Abdul it's time to go, we promised we would be home by 5 o'clock. We can come to the park tomorrow, **Insha Allah**," explained Yasmeen.

INSHA ALLAH - GOD WILLING

"Really, tomorrow," said an excited Abdul.

"Yes, **Insha Allah** we will come back tomorrow and play again," repeated Yasmeen.

"Promise me Yasmeen.
You have to promise me
that we will come back tomorrow.

You only keep on saying **Insha Allah**,"
complained Abdul.

"I can't promise you 100 percent that we will
come back tomorrow," Yasmeen
tried to explain to her brother.

"I'll explain when we get home,
now it's time to go, it's getting late,"
added Yasmeen.

"Sorry, we have to go home right now," said Abdul to Tasneem and Rafi.

"Will we see you both tomorrow?" asked Rafi.
"**Insha Allah**," answered Yasmeen.

When Yasmeen and
Abdul returned home,
both their parents were
waiting for them.

"Assalamu Alaikum," said Yasmeen and Abdul as they approached the house.
"Wa Alaikum Salam," replied their parents, happy to see them home again.
ASSALAMU ALAIKUM - PEACE BE UPON YOU
WA ALAIKUM SALAM - AND PEACE BE UPON YOU

"What took you so long?" asked their concerned mother.

"Sorry we were playing with Tasneem and Rafi
and having such a good time.
Sorry we took so long,"
apologized Abdul.

"That's ok, it was just a few minutes late, now both of you go inside and have a shower before we eat," said their father.

"Can I ask you a question?" asked Abdul.

"Of course you can, what is it?" replied his mother.

"At the park, Yasmeen kept on saying, **Insha Allah**, that we will come back to the park tomorrow.

But she wouldn't promise me.

Why did she keep on saying **Insha Allah** and wouldn't promise me?" asked a frustrated Abdul.

"Abdul, we never know what will happen to us tomorrow. Maybe something happens and you can't go to the park, that's why we say **Insha Allah**.

Allah tells us in the Qur'an:
*And never say of anything, Indeed, I will do that tomorrow, Except [when adding], If Allah wills (**Insha Allah**)...* *

It's up to the will of Allah if you will go to the park tomorrow," explained Abdul's mother patiently.

* Surah Number 18, Kahf (The Cave) Verse 23 & 24

"Aaah... Now I understand," said a very happy Abdul.

"From now on I will say **Insha Allah** for everything I want to do," added Abdul.

"But don't say **Insha Allah** for bad things," reminded his mother.

Abdul's father then came to the room.

"Do you still want to come with me to the mosque tonight Abdul?" asked his father.

"**Insha Allah**," said a proud and confident Abdul, with his new understanding of when to say **Insha Allah**.